THE ALMIGHTY BIBLE

A BIBLICALLY ACCURATE GRAPHIC NOVEL

S0-BMS-644

"I will call on Yahweh, who is worthy to be praised.
So shall I be saved from my enemies." (22:4)

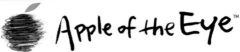

Apple of the Eye Publishing
© 2011 Dakedojo Grace, LLC
All rights reserved.

www.thealmightybible.com

The Almighty Bible is proudly marketed by

Your Full Service Christian Media Partner
1-800-974-1555
6000 Industrial Drive, Greenville, TX 75402
www.casscommedia.com

Printed in the USA
Produced by Golden Dog, My Legacy Press, and Dakedojo Grace.
Illustrations by Windbell Studiosh supervised by Sara Han-Williams – Pixtrend
Book Design by Poets Road

No portion of this book may be reprinted for commercial purposes or copied
with the intent of distributing it for free without the written consent of Dakedojo Grace, LLC.

Foreword

"As for God, His way is perfect. The Word of Yahweh is tested. He is a shield to all those who take refuge in Him. For who is God, besides Yahweh? Who is a rock, besides our God? God is my strong fortress. He makes my way perfect." (22:31-33)

Second Samuel follows directly upon the completion of First Samuel, with the two books occurring sometime between 1100 BC and 970 BC. Second Samuel is one of the 12 historical books in the Old Testament. The historical books come after the Pentateuch, and they begin with the conquest of the Promised Land under Joshua and lead up to Israel's restoration after the Babylonian captivity.

Whereas First Samuel delves significantly into the lives of Samuel and Saul, Second Samuel is devoted entirely to David's 40-year reign as king. The book also portrays an in-depth look at the close relationship between David and Yahweh, which is characterized by devotion, love, forgiveness, as well as betrayal and pain.

Second Samuel opens up with a bloody battle between the house of Saul and the house of David. Abner, the fierce leader of Saul's army, marches up to Gibeon to fight against Joab, the commander of David's army. The battle is severe, and many lives are lost among the men of Israel. When Abner runs away in defeat, Asahel, Joab's brother (who is as fast as a wild gazelle) (2:18), pursues after him. In spite of several warnings made by Abner, Asahel refuses to turn back. Abner then turns and kills Asahel in order to save himself; and so begins the blood feud between Abner and Joab.

During the long war between the house of Saul and David, David grows stronger and stronger while the house of Saul grows weaker and weaker (3:1).

Ultimately, the house of Saul fractures by itself when Ishbosheth, the son of Saul, rebukes Abner for being with Rizpah, Saul's concubine. Abner is so infuriated by this rebuke that he makes an oath to "transfer the kingdom from the house of Saul and to set up the throne of David over Israel and Judah" (3:10). David gladly accepts Abner's alliance, however, Joab kills Abner in Hebron to avenge the death of his brother Asahel. David is grief-stricken and laments deeply for the death of Abner. David also remarks on the blood-thirsty nature of Joab and his brothers, which is a recurring theme within Second Samuel: "The sons of Zeruiah are too hard for me. May Yahweh reward the evildoer according to his wickedness" (3:39).

After David is made king over the United Kingdom of Israel, he defeats the Jebusites and takes the mighty fortress of Jerusalem as his capital city. David also defeats the neighboring Philistines at Baal Perazim and the valley of Rephaim. In each battle, David inquires of Yahweh whether He will deliver his enemies into his hand and also gives praise after every victory: "Yahweh has broken my enemies before me, like the breach of waters" (5:20); "For You have armed me with strength for the battle. You have subdued under me those who rose up against me" (22:40).

David longs to have the Ark of the Covenant near him in Jerusalem. After a great ordeal that involved the death of Uzzah, a soldier who accidentally touches the Ark, and the sacrificing of an ox and calf every six paces as the soldiers carried the Ark, David is able to bring the Ark into Jerusalem. As the Ark enters the city David dances with all his might in front of the Ark, and his people, while wearing a linen ephod that left his body exposed for all to see. (6:14). So peculiar is his zeal in bringing the Ark to Jerusalem, that Michal, his first wife, "despised him in her heart" (6:16) as she watched him through her window. When David returns home, she remarks rather sarcastically about how he shamed himself, to which David famously answers he will be even more vile and base to celebrate before Yahweh (6:21). From that day forward, David avoids seeing Michal, and she never bears a child.

David plans on building a temple to house the Ark, but Yahweh sends the prophet Nathan to instruct David to leave the Ark in the tabernacle tent: "Shall you build me a house for me to dwell in? For I have not lived in a house since the day that I brought up the children of Israel out of Egypt, even to this day, but have moved around in a tent and in a tabernacle" (7:5-6). As disappointed as David must have been to hear this, God follows with an extraordinary promise and everlasting blessing: "I will set up your seed after you, who shall proceed out of your bowels, and I will establish his kingdom. He shall build a house for my name, and I will establish the throne of his kingdom forever" (7:12-13).

David then goes back to battle, subduing many nations including the Philistines, Moabites, Syrians, Edomites, and Ammonites. He dedicates all the silver and gold from these nations to Yahweh, and Yahweh gives victory to David wherever he goes (8:14). Seeking to do what is right and keep his oath to his beloved friend Jonathan, David restores great honor and wealth to Mephibosheth, the son of Jonathan, whose feet are lame.

At the height of his power, David's reign is suddenly marked by his flaw as a human being. One evening, while walking on the roof of his palace, David spots a beautiful woman bathing. He inquires after her and finds out her name: Bathsheba, the wife of Uriah the Hittite. Uriah was one of David's 37 mighty men (23:39) who was regarded highly enough to live very close to David's palace. Even after discovering that Bathsheba was the wife of one of his most loyal and skilled warriors, David decides to summon her. Later, Bathsheba sends David a message that she is pregnant with his child. Feeling guilty, David does everything in his power to have Uriah believe that Bathsheba is pregnant with his own child, but David's elaborate plans fails as Uriah continually reveals how exceptionally loyal he is to David: "The Ark, Israel, and Judah are staying in tents; and my lord Joab and the servants of my lord are encamped in the open field. Shall I then go into my house to eat and to drink and to lie with my life? As you live, and as your soul lives, I will not do this thing!" (11:11). David's guilt must have weighed even more heavily upon hearing such a commendable reply. Ultimately, David resorts to having his faithful soldier killed on the battlefield.

Yahweh does not let David's sin go unpunished. The prophet Nathan comes to David and recounts a story of a rich man who steals the only lamb of a poor man to prepare a feast for a traveler. David is outraged and says, "As Yahweh lives, the man who has done this is worthy to die!" (12:5). In a breathtaking, dramatic moment, Nathan accuses David of being the man who is worthy to die: "You are the man. You have struck Uriah the Hittite with the sword and have taken his wife to be your wife" (12:7-9). It is here that God's unwavering justice is revealed in full force: not only will the first son of David and Bathsheba die, God says that He will "raise up evil" (12:11) within David's own household and have another man lie with his wives in plain sight before all Israel (12:12). Later on, Absalom fulfills this prophecy.

The latter half of David's reign is filled with hardship and betrayal. His son Amnon commits a treacherous act against his half-sister, and Amnon is murdered by another son of David's, Absalom. Then, Absalom leads a rebellion that intends to overthrow and destroy David. So powerful is Absalom that David and his household flee from Jerusalem, his flight reminiscent of the time when King Saul sought to have him killed—only now his own son wants to kill him! Yet through all this, David holds steadfastly onto Yahweh and remains humble to the point of letting Shimei, a man of the house of Saul, curse and throw stones at him. When Abishai, brother of Joab and son of Zeruiah, requests David's permission to kill Shimei, David reprimands Abishai: "What have I do to with you, you sons of Zeruiah? He curses because Yahweh has said to him, 'Curse David.' Leave him alone and let him curse." (16:10-11).

Absalom's conspiracy is overthrown with the help of Hushai, the wise friend of David, and David returns to Jerusalem with a broken heart over the death of his son Absalom. However, David faces even greater hardships upon his return. When David decides to take a census in order to know the size of his army, God uses this event to bring a deadly pestilence on Israel, which kills 70,000 men (24:15). However, Yahweh prevents the pestilence from spreading to the appointed time and has David build an altar at the threshing floor of Araunah the Jebusite, which is where the angel of God has stopped the pestilence from continuing. After David offers burnt offerings, Yahweh prevents the plague from further afflicting Israel and so ends Second Samuel.

Although David was a man who committed evil in the sight of God, he was always quick to repent, correct his ways, suffer God's punishment, and seek to restore peace and righteousness for himself and his people. It was to David that God made the promise to establish his throne forever, which is referred to again and again in the New Testament as a foreshadowing of the coming of the Messiah.

As a magnificent, flawed hero who was beloved by God, David teaches us many valuable truths regarding faith: that no matter how far we fall, God's mercy is available to us if we repent of our ways and seek His righteousness. David's innermost thoughts and turmoils are laid bare in this song from psalms: "Create in me a clean heart, O God. Renew a right spirit within me. Don't throw me from Your presence, and don't take Your holy Spirit from me. Restore to me the joy of Your salvation" (Psalm 51:10-12).

NOTE TO READERS, PARENTS AND TEACHERS

This is a graphic novelization of 2 Samuel. It is not the entire biblical version, and we have made edits so that the story is as clear as possible. The text in this book has been edited down from an original public domain translation called the World English Bible, which itself was based on a 1904 version of the American Standard Bible. The verse numbers for every page are at the end of the text, allowing for easy reference to the full text in whichever version of the Bible you prefer. Our goal is to encourage young readers to start reading the Bible. Once they do, we believe they will never stop.

2 SAMUEL

MAIN CHARACTERS

DAVID
The second king of Israel who was a gifted musician, poet, and warrior. God blessed him with many victories over his enemies and promised that his throne will be established forever.

JOAB
A brave, fearless warrior who was the commander of David's army. He played a crucial part in ending Absalom's rebellion against David. He had two brothers, Abishai and Asahel.

ABNER
The valiant, fierce commander of Saul's army who served Ishbosheth, the son of Saul. He later pledged loyalty to the house of David after he was rebuked by Ish-bosheth.

MEPHIBOSHETH
The son of Jonathan and grandson of Saul. He lost the ability to walk when his nurse dropped him as they fled for safety. David restored great honor to Mephibosheth and protected him.

MICHAL
The daughter of Saul who was married to David but then given to another man named Paltiel. She was brought back to David through Abner. Later, Michal despised David in her heart.

MAIN CHARACTERS

BATHSHEBA

The beautiful wife of Uriah. After David saw her bathing, he sent messengers to summon her. She was later married to David.

NATHAN

The prophet who rebuked David for committing adultery with Bathsheba. God also spoke to Nathan in a vision that David's throne will be established forever through his offspring.

TAMAR

The good-hearted, kind daughter of David and sister of Absalom. She was very beautiful. Amnon, her half-brother, was killed because of what he did to her.

ABSALOM

The son of David who was the most handsome man in the kingdom. After avenging Tamar by murdering his half-brother, Absalom led a great rebellion against his father David.

HUSHAI

A close friend to David, Hushai spied on Absalom by pretending to be his servant. Hushai prevented Absalom from quickly pursuing after David and secured Absalom's defeat.

2 SAMUEL

After the death of Saul, David returned to Ziklag from the slaughter of the Amalekites. On the third day, a man from Saul's camp came with his clothes torn and earth on his head. He fell to the earth and showed respect. David said, "Where do you come from?" He said, "I have escaped out of the camp of Israel." (1:1–1:3)

1

David said, "How did it go?" The man answered, "The people have fled from the battle, and many are dead. Saul and Jonathan are dead also." David asked, "How do you know that Saul and Jonathan are dead?" The young man said, "As I passed Mount Gilboa, I saw Saul leaning on his spear as the chariots and the horsemen were charging towards him." (1:4–1:6)

The young man continued, "He saw me and called to me to kill him before the enemy got him. So I did as he asked, and I took the crown that was on his head and the bracelet that was on his arm, and I have brought them here to my lord." Then David took hold of his clothes and tore them, as did the men who were with him. (1:7–1:11)

They mourned, wept, and fasted until evening for King Saul, for his son, Jonathan, and for the people of Yahweh. David said to the young man, "How were you not afraid to kill Yahweh's anointed?" Then David had one of his men kill the man. David said, "Your blood be on your head, for your mouth has testified against you, saying, 'I have slain Yahweh's anointed.'" (1:12–1:16)

It happened after this that David inquired of Yahweh, saying, "Shall I go up into any of the cities of Judah?" Yahweh said to him, "Go up to Hebron." So David went up there. He brought up his men who were with him, every man with his household. They lived in the cities of Hebron. (2:1–2:3)

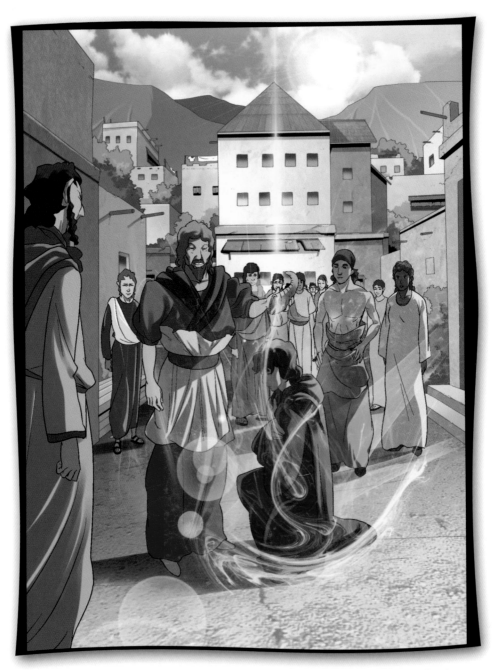

The men of Judah came, and there they anointed David king over the house of Judah. They then told David, "The men of Jabesh Gilead were the ones who buried Saul." David sent messengers to the men of Jabesh Gilead and said to them, "Blessed are you by Yahweh, that you have shown this kindness to your lord and have buried him." (2:4–2:5)

Now Abner the son of Ner, captain of Saul's army, had taken Ishbosheth the son of Saul and brought him over to Mahanaim, and he made him king over Gilead and over all Israel. Ishbosheth was forty years old when he began his two-year reign. But the house of Judah followed David as their king for seven years and six months. (2:8–2:11)

Abner rode out from Mahanaim to Gibeon to meet Joab the son of Zeruiah and the servant of David. They and their men went out and stopped at the pool of Gibeon. There they sat down, Abner and his men on one side, Joab and his men on the other side of the pool. Abner said to Joab, "Please let the young men arise and compete before us!" Joab said, "Let them arise!" (2:12–2:14)

Each side chose twelve young men. They each caught his opponent by the head and thrust his sword in his fellow's side; so they fell down dead together. To this day, they call this place the Field of Sharp Swords. The battle then broke out and was very severe that day as Abner and his men were defeated by Joab and the servants of David. (2:15–2:17)

Joab's two brothers, Abishai, and Asahel, were there with him. Asahel was as light of foot as a wild gazelle, and he ran after Abner and his men faster than all the others, who followed along a distance back. Abner yelled a warning back to Asahel, "Turn back and stop following me. I do not wish to kill you. How then could I hold up my face to Joab your brother?" (2:18–2:22)

However, Asahel refused to turn back, and he drew closer. Abner thrust the back end of his spear into Asahel's body, so that the spear came out behind him. Asahel fell down and died. Those that were following all stopped when they came to the body of Asahel. (2:23)

Joab then led everyone on in pursuit. Abner finally stopped on the hill of Ammah with his men behind him. He called to Joab and said, "Shall the sword devour forever? How long before your people stop pursuing their brothers?" So Joab blew the trumpet; he and his men turned back. They picked up Asahel's body and buried him in the tomb of his father in Bethlehem. They then returned to Hebron. (2:24–2:32)

Now there was a war between the house of Saul and the house of David. David grew stronger as the house of Saul grew weaker. Sons were born to David in Hebron: his firstborn was Amnon, of Ahinoam, and his second, Chileab, of Abigail the wife of Nabal, and the third, Absalom the son of Maacah, and the fourth, Adonijah the son of Haggith, and the fifth, Shephatiah the son of Abital, and the sixth, Ithream, of Eglah. (3:1–3:5)

Saul had a concubine whose name was Rizpah, whom Abner spent the night with, so Ishbosheth said to Abner, "Why have you gone in to my father's concubine?" Abner said, "Today I show kindness to the house of Saul and have not delivered you into the hand of David and yet you charge me with this! Now I swear to God that I shall help transfer the kingdom from the house of Saul to the house of David." (3:7–3:10)

Abner sent messengers to David on his behalf, saying, "Make your alliance with me, and behold, my hand shall be with you, to bring all Israel around to you." David said, "Good. I will make a treaty with you, but one thing I require of you: you shall not see my face, unless you first bring Michal, Saul's daughter, when you come to see me." (3:11–3:13)

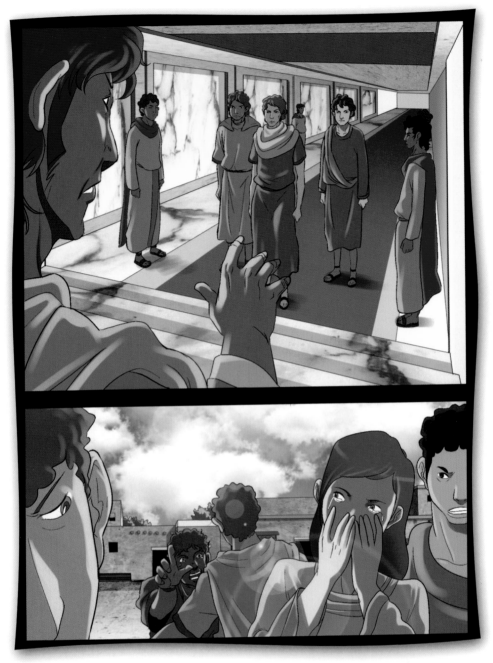

David sent messengers to Ishbosheth, Saul's son, saying, "Deliver me my wife Michal, whom I pledged to be married to me for one hundred foreskins of the Philistines." Ishbosheth took Michal from her husband, Paltiel. Paltiel, who loved her deeply, went with her, weeping, and followed her to Bahurim. Then Abner said to him, "Go! Return!" and he returned. (3:14–3:16)

Abner told the elders of Israel, "In times past, you sought for David to be king. Now then do it; for Yahweh has spoken of David, saying, 'By the hand of my servant David, I will save my people Israel out of the hand of the Philistines and out of the hand of all their enemies.'" Then Abner went to speak with David in Hebron on all he had been told. (3:17–3:19)

So Abner and twenty of his best men came to David in Hebron. David made a feast for Abner and the men who were with him. Abner said to David, "I will arise and go, and I will gather all Israel to my lord the king, that they may make a covenant with you and that you may reign over all that your soul desires." David sent Abner away in peace. (3:20–3:21)

Then Joab came to the king and said, "What have you done? Behold, Abner came to you, but you have sent him away free? You know Abner came to deceive you and to learn of all your defenses and weaknesses." When Joab left David, he sent messengers after Abner, and they brought him back from the well of Sirah, but David didn't know that Joab had done this. (3:24–3:26)

When Abner was brought back to Hebron, Joab took him aside beneath the gate to speak with him quietly and struck him there in the body and killed him as revenge for the blood of Asahel, Joab's brother. Afterward, when David heard it, he said, "I and my kingdom are guiltless before Yahweh forever of the blood of Abner." (3:27–3:30)

David said to Joab and to all the people who were with him, "Tear your clothes and mourn for Abner." They buried Abner in Hebron. King David lifted up his voice and wept, as did all the people. The king said, "Should Abner die as a fool dies? Your hands were not bound, nor your feet. As a man falls before wicked men, so you fell." All the people wept again over him. (3:31–3:34)

The people tried to get David to eat, but David swore, "God kill me if I eat before the sun sets." So all the people understood that day that it was not David who killed Abner. David said, "Don't you know that a prince and a great man has fallen this day? I am weak, and these sons of Zeruiah are too hard for me. May Yahweh reward them according to their wickedness." (3:35–3:39)

When Ishbosheth, Saul's son, heard that Abner was dead, his hands became feeble, and all the Israelites were troubled. Now Ishbosheth had a nephew, Jonathan's son, whose feet were lame because of a bad fall he'd experienced when his nurse was trying to flee with him after Saul and Jonathan's death. His name was Mephibosheth. (4:1–4:4)

When Ishbosheth took his rest at noon, two brothers, Rechab and Baanah, came into the house as he lay on his bed. They struck him and beheaded him. They brought the head of Ishbosheth to David in Hebron and said to the king, "Behold, the head of Ishbosheth, the son of Saul, your enemy, who sought your life! Yahweh has avenged my lord the king this day of Saul and of his seed." (4:5–4:8)

David answered the two brothers, "As Yahweh lives, when someone told me, 'Saul is dead,' thinking to have brought good news, I took hold of him and killed him as the reward I gave him for his news. How much more, when wicked men have slain a righteous person in his own house?" David commanded that the two men be killed. They then buried the head of Ishbosheth in the grave of Abner. (4:9–4:12)

Then all the tribes of Israel came to David at Hebron, saying, "Behold, Yahweh said to you, 'You shall be shepherd of my people Israel, and you shall be prince over Israel.'" So all the elders of Israel and David made a covenant before Yahweh, and they anointed David king over Israel. David was thirty years old when he began to reign, and he reigned forty years. (5:1–5:4)

David led his army to Jerusalem to battle the Jebusites. They thought they were safe behind their walls, saying, "Even the blind and the lame could stop you." However, they were wrong. David took the city by sending his men in through the water channel, telling them to strike the lame and the blind, meaning the men and soldiers who had taunted David. (5:6–5:8)

David moved his household there and called it the City of David. David grew stronger and stronger, for Yahweh was with him. Hiram, king of Tyre, sent David cedar trees, carpenters, and masons to build David a house. David knew then that Yahweh had established him king over Israel and that his kingdom was exalted for the sake of Yahweh's people. (5:9–5:12)

Now the Philistines had come and spread throughout the valley of Rephaim. David prayed to God, asking, "Shall I go up against the Philistines? Will you deliver them into my hand?" Yahweh said to David, "Go up, for I will certainly deliver the Philistines into your hand." (5:18–5:19)

David came to Baal Perazim. Yahweh said, "Circle around behind them and attack them over against the mulberry trees. It shall be, when you hear the sound of marching in the tops of the mulberry trees, that then you shall move, for Yahweh has gone out before you to strike the army of the Philistines." David did so. (5:20–5:25)

David gathered thirty thousand chosen ones and went with them to bring up the Ark of God. They set the Ark of God on a new cart and brought it out of the house of Abinadab that was in the hill. Uzzah and Ahio, the sons of Abinadab, drove the new cart back to the City of David. David and others played before Yahweh with harps, wooden instruments, tambourines, and castanets. (6:1–6:5)

When they came to the threshing floor of Nacon, Uzzah reached for the Ark and took hold of it because the cattle stumbled. But the anger of Yahweh was kindled against Uzzah, and God struck him there for his error of touching that which was holy. Uzzah died by the Ark. David was troubled because of what Yahweh had done to Uzzah. (6:6–6:8)

David feared Yahweh, thinking that he should not move the Ark of Yahweh. David had the Ark taken to the house of Obed-Edom. A few months later, David was told, "Yahweh has blessed the house of Obed-Edom." Then David went and brought the Ark into the City of David. Sacrifices were made every few steps of the journey. (6:9–6:13)

As the Ark entered the city, David danced before Yahweh with all his might. David was clothed in a linen ephod that was very revealing. Michal the daughter of Saul looked out the window and saw David leaping and dancing before Yahweh with his clothing askew, and she despised him in her heart. (6:14–6:16)

They set the Ark in the tent that David had pitched for it. David made offerings before Yahweh and then blessed the people in the name of Yahweh. He gave to all the people a portion of bread, dates, and raisins. All the people then departed for their homes. (6:17–6:19)

When David returned to his household, Michal said, "How glorious the king of Israel was today, uncovering himself in the eyes of the handmaids!" David said, "It was before Yahweh who chose me above your father as prince over Israel. Therefore will I celebrate before Yahweh and will be base in my own sight." Michal had no child to the day of her death. (6:20–6:23)

One day, David said to Nathan the prophet, "I dwell in a house of cedar, but the Ark of God dwells within curtains." The same night, the word of Yahweh came to Nathan, saying, "Go and tell my servant David, 'Shall you build me a house for me to dwell in? For I have not lived in a house since I brought the children of Israel out of Egypt, but have moved around in a tent and in a tabernacle.'" (7:1–7:6)

"'Moreover, Yahweh will make you a house. When your days are fulfilled, I will set up your seed after you and establish his kingdom. He shall build a house for my name, and I will establish the throne of his kingdom forever. I will be his father, and he shall be my son. Your house and your kingdom shall be established forever.'" According to all these words, so Nathan spoke to David. (7:11–7:17)

Then David sat before Yahweh, saying, "Who am I, Lord, and what is my house, that You have brought me thus far? What more can David say to You? For You know Your servant, Lord. According to Your own heart, You have worked all this greatness, to make Your servant know it. Therefore You are great, God. For there is none like You, neither is there any God besides You. (7:18–7:22)

After this, it happened that David struck the Philistines and subdued them. David took control of the main city from them. He struck Moab and measured them with a line, making them lie down on the ground. He measured two lines to put to death and one full line to keep alive. The Moabites became servants to David and brought tribute. (8:1–8:2)

David struck also Hadadezer the son of Rehob, king of Zobah, as he went to recover his dominion at the River. David took from him one thousand seven hundred horsemen and twenty thousand footmen. David hamstrung all the chariot horses but kept one hundred chariots. (8:3–8:4)

When the Syrians of Damascus came to help Hadadezer king of Zobah, David killed two and twenty thousand men. Then David put garrisons in Syria, and the Syrians became servants to David and brought tribute. Yahweh gave victory to David wherever he went. David took the shields of gold that were on the servants of Hadadezer, and he brought them to Jerusalem. (8:5–8:7)

When Toi, king of Hamath, heard that David had struck Hadadezer, he sent Joram, his son, to greet and bless David because Toi had wars with Hadadezer as well. Joram brought vessels of silver, gold, and brass. King David dedicated these to Yahweh along with all of the other riches he had captured in his battles. (8:9–8:12)

He put garrisons in Edom, and the Edomites became David's servants. Yahweh gave victory to David wherever he went. David reigned over all Israel, and he executed justice and righteousness to all his people. Joab was over the army; Jehoshaphat was recorder; Zadok and Ahimelech were priests; Seraiah was scribe; Benaiah was over the Cherethites and Pelethites; and David's sons were chief ministers. (8:14–8:18)

David said, "Is there yet any who is left of the house of Saul that I may show him kindness for Jonathan's sake?" A servant named Ziba, who had served Saul, was brought to David. Ziba said, "Jonathan has a living son who has lame feet." The king said to him, "Where is he?" Ziba said, "Behold, he is in the house of Machir, in Lo Debar." (9:1–9:4)

Then king David sent and fetched Jonathan's son to him. When he came to David, the king fell on his face and showed respect. David said, "Mephibosheth, don't be afraid, for I will surely show you kindness for Jonathan your father's sake and will restore to you all the land of Saul your father. You shall eat bread at my table continually." Mephibosheth bowed down. (9:5–9:8)

Then the king called to Ziba and said, "All that pertained to Saul have I given to your master's son. You shall till the land for him, you, your sons, and your servants. You shall bring in the harvest, but Mephibosheth, your master's son, shall always eat bread at my table." Ziba, who had fifteen sons and twenty servants, said to the king, "All that my king commands, so your servant shall do." (9:9–9:11)

So Mephibosheth ate at the king's table like one of David's sons. Mephibosheth eventually had a son whose name was Mica. All that lived in the house of Ziba were servants to Mephibosheth. Mephibosheth lived in Jerusalem, for he ate continually at the king's table. He remained lame in both his feet. (9:12–9:13)

The king of Ammon died, and Hanun his son reigned. David said, "I will show kindness to Hanun, as his father showed kindness to me." So David sent his servants into the land of Ammon with good intent. But the princes of the children of Ammon said to Hanun, "Do you think that David honors your father or has David sent his servants to search the city for ways to overthrow it?" (10:1–10:3)

So Hanun took David's servants and shaved off one half of their beards and their clothing, and he sent them away. When they returned, David said, "Wait at Jericho until your beards have grown." In the meantime, Hanun hired twenty thousand Syrian footmen, one thousand men from Maacah, and twelve thousand men from Tob. When David heard of it, he sent Joab and all his mighty men. (10:4–10:7)

The Ammon army came out and waited outside the entrance of the city. The Syrians and the men of Tob and Maacah were by themselves in the field. When Joab saw that the battle was set against him before and behind, he chose the choice men of Israel and put them in array against the Syrians. The rest of the people he committed into the hand of Abishai his brother against the men of Ammon. (10:8–10:10)

Joab said to his brother, "If the Syrians are too strong for me, then you shall help me, but if the children of Ammon are too strong for you, then I will come and help you. Be courageous, and let us be strong for our people and for the cities of our God. May Yahweh do that which seems good to Him." (10:11–10:12)

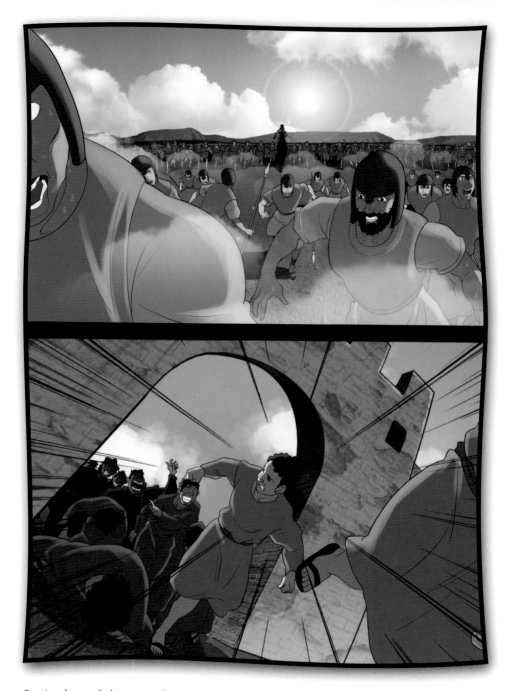

So Joab and the people who were with him advanced on the Syrians, and they fled before him. When the children of Ammon saw that the Syrians had fled, they likewise fled before Abishai and entered into the city. Then Joab returned to Jerusalem. When the Syrians saw that they were defeated by Israel, they gathered themselves together in Helam. (10:13–10:15)

David and his army fought the Syrians in Helam. The Syrians fled before Israel, and David's men killed seven hundred charioteers, forty thousand horsemen, and Shobach the captain of their army. When all the kings who were servants to Hadadezer saw that they were defeated by Israel, they made peace with King David and served him. So the Syrians helped the children of Ammon no more. (10:16–10:19)

It happened in the spring, at the time when kings go out to war, that Joab and the army went out, but David stayed in Jerusalem. One evening, David arose from his bed and walked on the roof of his palace. From the roof, he saw a woman bathing, and the woman was very beautiful to look upon. (11:1–11:2)

David inquired after the woman and was told by one person, "This is Bathsheba, the daughter of Eliam, the wife of Uriah the Hittite." David sent messengers, and she came to him. He lay with her, and then she returned to her house. (11:3–11:4)

Bathsheba told David, "I am with child." David's general, Joab, sent for Uriah. David said to Uriah, "Go down to your house and wash your feet." But Uriah slept at the door of the king's house, telling David that he could not go eat and drink and lie with his wife when the Ark and his fellow soldiers were in tents and fields. (11:5–11:11)

David said, "Stay here and tomorrow I will let you depart." So Uriah stayed in Jerusalem that day and the next. David served much food and drink, hoping Uriah would then go lie with Bathsheba. But at night, he still wouldn't go to his house. The next morning, David wrote to Joab, saying, "Send Uriah to the front of the hottest battle and retreat from him, that he may be struck and die." (11:12–11:15)

Joab sent Uriah to the place where he knew that valiant men were fighting, and Uriah was killed in battle. Then Joab sent a messenger to David, "The enemy prevailed against us, but we fought all the way to the entrance of the gate. Their shooters shot at your servants from off the wall, and some of the king's servants are dead, including Uriah the Hittite." (11:16–11:24)

When Bathsheba, the wife of Uriah, heard that her husband was dead, she mourned for him. When the mourning was past, David sent for her and took her into his house, and she became his wife and bore him a son. But the thing that David had done displeased Yahweh. (11:26–11:27)

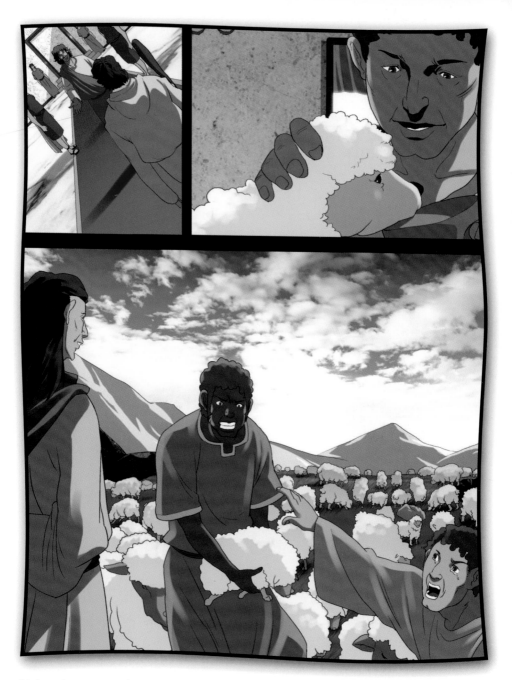

Yahweh sent Nathan, the prophet, to tell David, "There were two men, one rich and one poor. The rich man had many flocks and herds, but the poor man had nothing but one little ewe lamb. It grew up with his children and was to him like another child. A traveler came to the rich man, but instead of serving one of his many lambs to cook for the traveler, he took the poor man's lamb." (12:1–12:4)

David was angered by the rich man's actions and said to Nathan, "The man who has done this should die!" Nathan responded, "You are the man. This is what Yahweh says: 'I anointed you king over Israel and delivered you out of the hand of Saul. I gave you your master's house, and wives. Yet you have killed Uriah and have taken his wife. Now therefore, the sword will never depart from your house.'" (12:5–12:10)

Nathan continued, "This is what Yahweh says: 'Behold, I will take your wives and give them to your neighbor, and he will lie with them in plain sight. You did it secretly, but I will do this thing before all Israel.'" David said to Nathan, "I have sinned against Yahweh." Nathan said to David, "Yahweh also has put away your sin. You will not die. However, the child who is born to you shall surely die." (12:11–12:15)

Yahweh struck the child that Uriah's wife bore to David, and it was very sick. David begged God for the child. He fasted and lay all night on the earth. The elders of his house arose beside him, to raise him up from the earth, but he would not, neither did he eat bread with them. (12:15–12:17)

On the seventh day, the child died. David arose, washed, anointed himself, and came into the house of Yahweh, and he worshiped. Then he went home and ate, saying to his servants, "While the child was alive, I fasted and wept, for I said, 'Who knows whether Yahweh will be gracious to me and let the child live?' But now that he is dead, why should I fast? Can I bring him back again?" (12:18–12:23)

David comforted Bathsheba, his wife, and lay with her. She became pregnant and bore a second child, a son, and David named him Solomon. Yahweh loved Solomon. (12:24–12:25)

Now Joab fought against the city of Rabbah in the land of Ammon. Joab sent messengers to David, "I have fought against Rabbah. Yes, I have taken the city of waters. Now therefore, gather the rest of the people together and come so that you may enter the city first, lest it be called after my name." David gathered all the people together, and he went to Rabbah and took it. (12:26–12:29)

They took the gold and bejeweled crown from the head of their king, and it was set on David's head. He collected the riches of the city and put the children of Ammon to work with saws and picks. David did so to all the Ammonite cities, and then the children of Israel returned to Jerusalem. (12:30–12:31)

David's son, Absalom, had a beautiful sister whose name was Tamar, and Amnon, another son of David, loved her. Amnon had a cousin, Jonadab, the son of Shimeah. Jonadab said to him, "Why, son of the king, are you so sad?" Amnon said, "I love Tamar." Jonadab said, "Pretend to be sick. When your father comes, tell him, 'Please let my sister Tamar come and give me bread to eat.'" (13:1–13:5)

So, Amnon faked being sick. When David came to see him, Amnon said, "Please let Tamar come." So Tamar went to her brother Amnon's house. She took dough and kneaded it, and she made cakes in his sight. She took the pan and poured them out before him, but he refused to eat. Amnon said, "Have all men leave me." Everyone but Tamar left. (13:6–13:9)

Amnon said to Tamar, "Bring the food into the room, that I may eat from your hand." When she had brought them near to him to eat, he took hold of her and said, "Come, lie with me, me!" She answered him, "No, my brother, do not force me! For no such thing ought to be done in Israel. Instead, please speak to the king, for he will give me to you in marriage." (13:10–13:13)

However, he would not listen to her voice and forced her to lay with him. Then the hatred with which he hated her was greater than the love with which he had loved her. Amnon said to her, "Arise, be gone!" She said to him, "Not so, because this great wrong in sending me away is worse than the other that you did to me!" But he would not listen to her. (13:14–13:17)

Tamar put ashes on her head, and tore her garment of various colors, and she laid her hand on her head and went her way, crying aloud as she went. (13:19)

Absalom her brother said to her, "Has Amnon been with you? Do not worry, my sister. Don't take this thing to heart." But Tamar remained desolate in her brother Absalom's house. When David heard of all these things, he was very angry, and Absalom hated Amnon in his heart because he had forced himself upon Tamar. (13:20–13:22)

After two full years, Absalom came to the king and said, "Please let the king and his servants come with me for a celebration." David let Amnon and all the king's sons go with him. Absalom commanded his servants, saying, "When Amnon's heart is merry with wine and I tell you, 'Strike Amnon,' kill him." The servants of Absalom did to Amnon as Absalom had commanded. (13:23–13:29)

Then all the king's sons arose, and every man got up on his mule and fled. Before they returned to Jerusalem, rumors reached David, "Absalom has slain all the king's sons, and there is not one of them left!" Believing what he was told, David arose, tore his garments, and lay on the earth. All his servants stood by with their clothes torn. (13:29–13:31)

Jonadab, who had started the trouble, then told David that only Amnon was dead. Then Jonadab saw the king's sons approaching and said, "Behold, the king's sons are coming! It is as your servant said." As soon as he finished speaking, the king's sons came. The king wept bitterly for Amnon. (13:32–13:36)

Fearing for his life, Absalom fled and went to stay with his grandfather, Talmai, king of Geshur. David longed to go forth to Absalom, for he missed his son deeply and had already reconciled himself to the death of Amnon. However, David did not reach out to Absalom, leaving him in exile for three years. (13:37–13:39)

Now Joab knew that the king missed Absalom. Joab devised a plan and sent a wise woman in to David, pretending she was in mourning. When the woman spoke to the king, she fell to the ground, showed respect, and said, "Help, O king!" The king said to her, "What ails you?" She answered, "I am a widow with no one to turn to." (14:1–14:5)

"I had two sons, but they fought and one killed the other. Now my relatives want me to send my living son to them so they can kill him for his crime, leaving no one to care for me or carry on my husband's name." David responded, "Return home, and I will make a commandment that shall solve your problem." (14:6–14:9)

David continued, "Anyone who tries to harm your son, send them to me. As Yahweh lives, not one hair of your son shall fall to the earth." Then the woman said, "Thank you, my Lord, and may I speak further?" David said, "Say on." She said, "Your words are wise, but why then does the king not bring home his own banished son?" (14:10–14:13)

David knew immediately that he had been tricked and asked, "Did Joab send you?" The woman answered, "Yes, my Lord." The king then said to Joab, "You are right. Go therefore and bring Absalom back." Joab fell to the ground and blessed the king. Then Joab arose and went to Geshur to retrieve Absalom. (14:19–14:23)

And Joab brought Absalom to Jerusalem. (14:23)

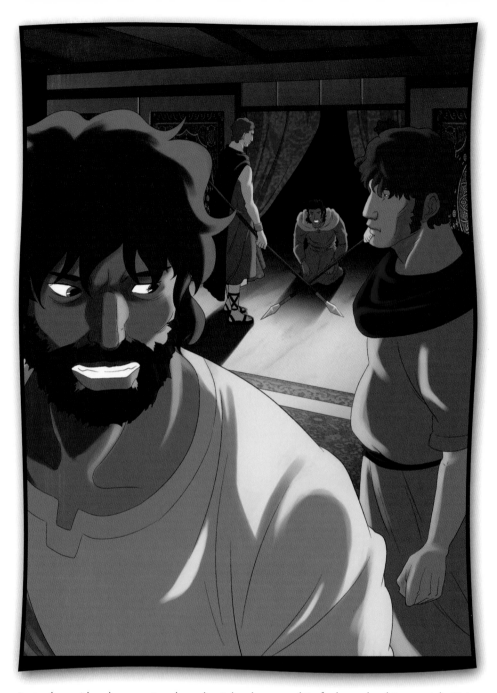

But when Absalom arrived and wished to see his father, the king said, "No, let my son return to his own house. Because of what he has done, he shall not see my face." So Absalom returned to his own house, and he waited. (14:24)

While Absalom waited, the people marveled at how handsome he was. His hair was long and thick, and his face was becoming. For two years, Absalom waited without seeing his father's face. Finally, tired of waiting, Absalom sent for Joab to demand that his father see him, but Joab would not come to him.. (14:25–14:29)

Then Absalom told his servants, "Joab's barley field is near mine. Go and set it on fire." Absalom's servants did so, and Joab went in anger to see Absalom, "Why have you done this thing?" Absalom answered, "Because you would not come see me. Why have I come from Geshur? It would be better for me to be there still. Now let me see my father. If he still finds fault in me, let him kill me." (14:30–14:32)

So Joab came to David and told him what Absalom had done and said. Finally, David agreed to see his son and called for him to come to his palace. Absalom came to the king, and bowed with his face to the ground before the king. Forgiving his son, David kissed Absalom. (14:33)

Soon after this, Absalom began traveling in a chariot with fifty men accompanying him. They would wait at the city gates each morning and tell the people who came to see the king for judgment that it was unfortunate that he was not the judge because their case seemed righteous to him. He would then kiss their hand, and the people began to favor Absalom. (15:1–15:5)

So Absalom eventually stole the hearts of the men of Israel. After many years of doing this, Absalom said to David, "Please let me go to Hebron and worship God. For your servant vowed a vow while I stayed at Geshur in Syria, saying, 'If Yahweh shall indeed bring me again to Jerusalem, then I will serve Yahweh.'" David said to him, "Go in peace." So Absalom arose and went to Hebron. (15:6–15:9)

But Absalom sent spies throughout Israel, saying, "When you hear the sound of the trumpet, you shall say, 'Absalom is king!'" Two hundred men went with Absalom out of Jerusalem, but they did not know his plans. Absalom sent for Ahithophel, David's counselor, while he was offering the sacrifices in Hebron. The conspiracy was soon spread across all of Israel, for the people loved Absalom. (15:10–15:12)

David learned of Absalom's treason and said to the people of Jerusalem, "Arise and let us flee quickly before Absalom returns and destroys us." The king's servants said to the king, "Behold, your servants are ready to do whatever my lord the king chooses." The king went forth and all his household after him. But David left ten women who were his concubines to care for his palace. (15:14–15:16)

The king went forth and all the people after him. They stayed in Beth Merhak. All the country wept with a loud voice as they continued their journey. They came to the brook at Kidron, and everyone crossed it, including the king. They then headed into the wilderness with heavy hearts. (15:17–15:23)

The priests, Abiathar and Zadok, also came, as well as the Levites who brought the Ark of the Covenant. But David said to Zadok, "Carry back the Ark into the city. If I find favor in the eyes of Yahweh, He will bring me back to see it again. I will stay at the fords of the wilderness, waiting word from you as to what happens in Jerusalem." (15:24–15:29)

David then led the people up the Mount of Olives and wept as he walked. He had his head covered and went barefoot, and all the people who were with him covered their heads and wept as well. Someone told David, "Ahithophel, your advisor, is among the conspirators with Absalom." David prayed, "Yahweh, please turn the counsel of Ahithophel into foolishness." (15:30–15:31)

It happened that when David had come to the top where God was worshiped, behold, Hushai came to meet him. David said to him, "Return to the city and tell Absalom that you will be his servant so that you may give him false counsel. Tell what you learn to Zadok and Abiathar the priests. Their two sons, Ahimaaz and Jonathan, will run to me with everything that you shall hear." (15:32–15:36)

So Hushai returned to Jerusalem as Absalom entered it. Back on the Mount of Olives, Ziba, the servant of Mephibosheth, met David with bags of food and jugs of wine. The king said, "Where is Mephibosheth?" Ziba said, "Behold, he is in Jerusalem hoping that he will be placed as king because he is the son of Saul." David then decreed that all that was Mephibosheth's should now be Ziba's. (15:37–16:4)

When David came to Bahurim, behold, a man named Shimei, of the family of the house of Saul, came out and cursed David for all of the evil he had done to King Saul. Shimei cast stones at David and at all who traveled with David, saying, "Yahweh has delivered the kingdom into the hand of Absalom your son! Behold, you are caught by your own mischief because you are a man of blood!" (16:5–16:7)

Then Abishai, Joab's brother, said to David, "Why should this dead dog curse my lord the king? Please let me go over and take off his head." The king said, "Why are you and your brother so anxious to kill people? Yahweh has said to him, 'Curse David,' so who are we to kill this man?" (16:8–16:10)

David then said to Abishai and to all his servants, "Behold, my own son seeks my life. Leave this man alone, and let him curse. Perhaps Yahweh will take pity and do good unto His servant for the cursing of me today." So David and his men ignored Shimei until he finally stopped following them. Finally, David and his followers reached the Jordan River and refreshed themselves. (16:11–16:14)

Meanwhile, in Jerusalem, Hushai said to Absalom, "Long live the king!"
Absalom said to Hushai, "Why didn't you go with your friend, my father? Is
this how you repay him?" Hushai said to Absalom, "Whomever Yahweh and
the men of Israel have chosen, his will I be, and with him I will stay. Shouldn't
I serve you as I have served your father?" (16:15–16:19)

Then Absalom asked the traitor, Ahithophel, what he should do now that he had taken Jerusalem. Ahithophel said to Absalom, "Go in to your father's ten concubines and shame your father." So Absalom went in to his father's concubines in the sight of all Israel. (Thus, were the words of God fulfilled regarding the evil that David had done to the husband of Bathsheba.) (16:20–16:23)

Ahithophel then advised Absalom to take twelve thousand soldiers so that he may go and kill David that very day while he was close and exhausted from the journey. This way he could kill David but leave those who traveled with David alive so that they would come back to serve Absalom and live in peace. Absalom and the elders thought this wise, but before agreeing, Absalom sent for Hushai. (17:1–17:6)

Hushai counseled otherwise, "You know your father and his mighty men. They are fierce men of war, and David will hide while his soldiers kill some of your men. Then word will spread that Absalom's soldiers are losing, and the hearts of your followers will melt in fear of the great David. Instead, gather to you a huge army and lead them yourself. We will then find him and destroy him and all who are with him." (17:7–17:13)

Absalom and the elders said, "The counsel of Hushai is better than the counsel of Ahithophel." Then Hushai said to Zadok and to Abiathar the priests, "Now therefore send word quickly and tell David, 'Don't lodge this night at the fords of the wilderness, but by all means pass over lest the king be swallowed up and all the people who are with him.'" (17:14–17:16)

Now Jonathan and Ahimaaz, the sons of the priests, slipped away as quickly as possible to go on their mission. However, they were seen by a boy who then told Absalom about them. Jonathan and Ahimaaz knew they would soon be followed. They raced to the home of a man they knew in Bahurim. They hid in his well. (17:17–17:18)

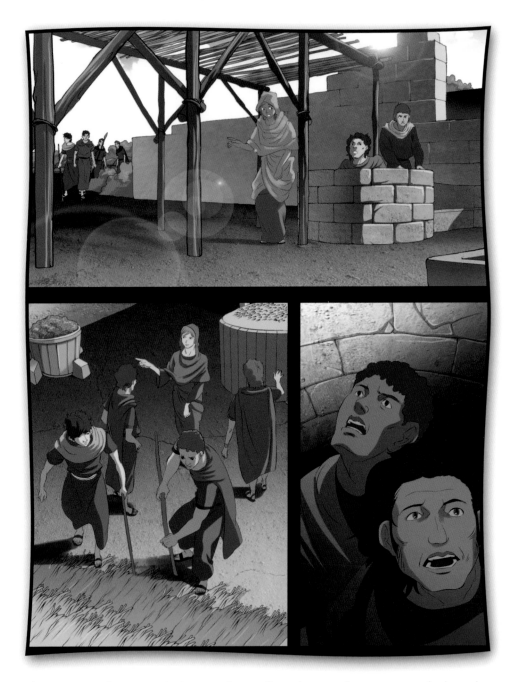

The man's wife put a cloth over the well and spread grain on it, hiding the well from sight. Absalom's soldiers soon came to the woman to the house, and they said, "Where are Ahimaaz and Jonathan?" The woman said to them, "They have gone that way, over the brook." The soldiers rode off in pursuit, believing the woman. (17:19–17:20)

Ahimaaz and Jonathan came up out of the well, and they went and told King David, "Arise and pass quickly over the water, for thus has Ahithophel counseled against you." Then David arose and all the people who were with him, and they passed over the Jordan during the night and continued their journey until they came to Mahanaim. (17:21–17:22)

Back in Jerusalem, Absalom drew to him men from all of Israel, and when he had brought together a huge army, they set out in pursuit of David. Absalom set Amasa over the army, taking the place of Joab, who remained loyal to David. After crossing the Jordan, Israel and Absalom encamped in the land of Gilead. (17:24–17:26)

David set Abishai, Joab and a third general, Ittai the Gittite, in charge of his army. David was ready to lead them all, but the people begged him to stay hidden in the city. The king said to them, "I will do what seems best to you." The king stood beside the gate, and all the people went out by hundreds and by thousands. (18:1–18:4)

The king commanded Joab, Abishai, and Ittai in front of all the people, "For my sake, deal gently with my son, Absalom." So the people went out into the forests of Ephraim and waited for Absalom's army to arrive. The forests and the soldiers of David were equally ferocious and twenty thousand of Absalom's men were killed in the battle. (18:5–18:8)

Absalom was riding on his mule, trying to escape some of David's soldiers when his head hit a branch, and he was left dangling in the air. Knowing what David had said, the men held Absalom while they got Joab. Joab asked why they had not killed Absalom, and they again recited David's wish to keep him safe. (18:9–18:13)

Then Joab said, "I'm not going to wait like this with you." He took three spears in his hand and thrust them through the heart of Absalom. Ten young men who bore Joab's armor then surrounded and struck Absalom until he was dead. Joab blew the trumpet, and the people returned from pursuing after Israel and stopped the killing, now that Absalom was dead. (18:14–18:16)

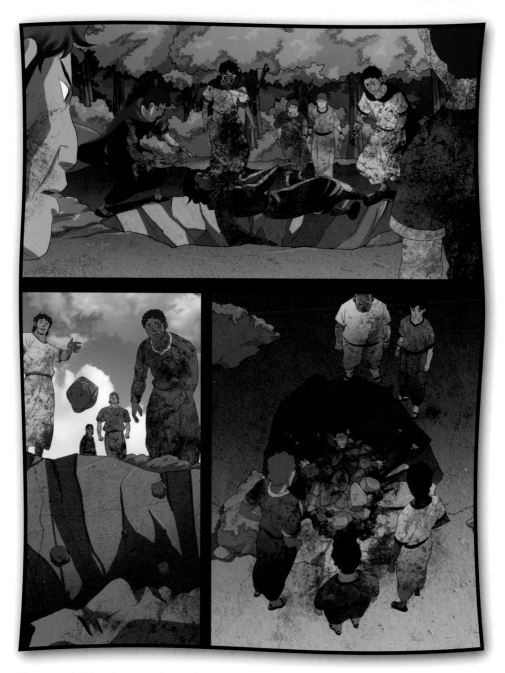

They took Absalom and cast him into a pit and covered him with rocks. Then his followers all fled back to their homes. Ahimaaz said to Joab, "Let me now run and bear the king news." Joab, concerned as to how David would treat a messenger bringing such news, said to him, "You shall not be the bearer of news this day because the king's son is dead." (18:17–18:20)

Then Joab said to another runner, "Go, tell the king what you have seen!" The man bowed and ran. Ahimaaz pleaded with Joab, "Come what may, please let me also run." Joab said, "Why do you want to run, my son, since the reward may not be good?" Ahimaaz repeated, "Come what may, I will run." Joab finally agreed and Ahimaaz ran by the way of the Plain and outran the other man. (18:21–18:23)

Back in the city, the watchman cried out to the king. David said, "If he is alone, he carries news." He came closer and closer. The watchman said, "I think that he runs like Ahimaaz the son of Zadok." The king said, "Ahimaaz is a good man and comes with good news." (18:24–18:27)

Ahimaaz called out to David, "All is well." He bowed and said, "Blessed is God who has delivered up the men who lifted up their hand against you!" The king said, "And how is Absalom?" Ahimaaz answered, "I saw a great tumult, but I do not know." Just then, the other runner arrived and said, "Yahweh has avenged you this day." David asked him about Absalom as well. The man answered, "He too is dead." (18:28–18:32)

The king was overcome with emotion and went up to the room over the gate and wept. As he went, he said, "My son Absalom! My son, my son Absalom! I wish I had died for you, Absalom, my son, my son!" Word of this reached Joab, "Behold, the king weeps and mourns for Absalom." Joab was upset that the day of victory was turned into a day of mourning as the news reached the people. (18:33–19:2)

The people returned and listened to their king mourn, "My son Absalom, my son!" Joab came to David and said, "You have shamed your servants who have saved your life and the lives of your offspring. You love those who hate you and hate those who love you. For today I perceive that if Absalom had lived and we had died, then it would have pleased you well." (19:3–19:6)

Joab said, "Now arise and speak to your people, for if you don't, not a man will stay with you after this night." Then the king arose, and the people came to him. But those who had followed Absalom returned home in turmoil, saying, "The king delivered us out of the hand of our enemies, and he saved us from the Philistines; now he has fled Jerusalem because of Absalom, whom we anointed over us. But Absalom is dead and why is David not again our king?" (19:7–19:10)

David heard the words of the people and sent Zadok and Abiathar to go speak to the elders of Judah and ask them, "Why are you the last to say it is time to bring the king back to his house?" David told them to tell his nephew, Amasa, that he would appoint him general over Joab. The priests did as they were told, and they convinced the elders of Judah to call for David's return, as king.(19:11–19:14)

So Shimei, who had cursed David and his soldiers, hurried down with the men of Judah and fell down before the king, saying, "Don't let my lord remember that which I did the day that my lord the king went out of Jerusalem. For I know that I have sinned. Therefore behold, I have come this day the first of all the house of Joseph to go down to meet my lord the king and ask forgiveness." (19:15–19:20)

But Abishai answered, "Shall Shimei not be put to death?" David said, "What have I to do with you, you sons of Zeruia?" The king said to Shimei, "You shall not die." Then Mephibosheth the son of Saul came down to meet the king, and he had neither trimmed his beard nor washed his clothes from the day the king departed. David said to him, "Why didn't you go with me, Mephibosheth?" (19:21–19:25)

He answered, "O king, my servant Ziba deceived me. He told me he was preparing a donkey for me but then left me lame and unable to follow. But my lord is as wise as an angel. Do therefore what is good in your eyes." The king said to him, "Why do you speak any more of such matters? I say, you and Ziba divide the land." Mephibosheth said to the king, "It is enough that you are safe, let him have it all." (19:26–19:30)

Barzillai the Gileadite was eighty years old, and he had provided David with food while he stayed at Mahanaim, for he was a great man. David said to Barzillai, "Come with me to Jerusalem." But Barzillai said, "I am too old to go with you, but let my servant Chimham go with my lord the king." David answered, "Chimham shall go with me. For whatever you require of me, that I will do for you." (19:31–19:38)

All the people with David crossed the Jordan. David said goodbye to Barzillai, kissing and blessing him, and Barzillai returned to his own home while his servant Chimham crossed the Jordan with David. Waiting to return to Jerusalem with David was the full army of Judah and half of the army of Israel. (19:39–19:40)

Behold, jealousy arose and the soldiers of Israel asked David why he should be surrounded by the soldiers of Judah. The soldiers of Judah replied, "Because the king is a close relative to us. Why are you angry? We have not taken his food or riches." The men of Israel answered, "King David belongs to us ten times more than you. We were the first ones to say he should be returned as king." A Benjamite named Sheba blew the trumpet and said, "If David does not belong to us, then let us return home!" (19:41–20:1)

So the men of Israel followed Sheba while the men of Judah escorted David from the Jordan to Jerusalem. David came to his house and had his ten concubines moved to a new home where they were given what they needed, but he never again went to them so that they lived their remaining days as if they were widows. (20:2–20:3)

Then David told Amasa to amass the army in three days to pursue Sheba. However, Amasa took too long, and David sent Abishai and Joab out with his personal bodyguards and best soldiers. When they were at the great stone that is in Gibeon, Amasa came to meet them. Joab approached Amasa as if to greet him, but in his hand he held his sword. (20:4–20:8)

Joab said to Amasa, "Is it well with you, my brother?" Joab took Amasa by the beard as if to kiss him. But instead Joab struck Amasa with the sword in the stomach and killed him. Joab and Abishai then continued their pursuit of Sheba. One of their young soldiers yelled out to the followers of Amasa, "He who favors Joab and he who is for David, let him follow Joab!" (20:9–20:11)

However, many men stood staring at their fallen leader until Amasa was moved to the side of the road and covered with a garment. Then the soldiers moved forward and followed Joab in his pursuit for Sheba. (20:12–20:13)

Sheba went through the tribes of Israel before he stopped in the town of Abel Beth-Maacah. There he was met by his best soldiers who followed him into the town. Joab and his troops soon arrived and surrounded the city walls so none could enter or leave. They made a battering ram and prepared to break open the gates of the city. (20:14–20:15)

Then a wise woman cried out, "Hear, hear. I am among those who are peaceable and faithful in Israel. Why do you seek to destroy a city of Israel?" Joab answered, "Far be it from me that I should swallow up or destroy your city. Sheba has lifted up his hand against the king. Deliver him to us, and we will depart from the city." The woman said, "Behold, his head shall be thrown to you over the wall." (20:16–20:21)

Then the woman went to all the people and told them of what Joab had promised. They cut off the head of Sheba and threw it out to Joab. Joab immediately had a man blow the trumpet, and his soldiers immediately stopped their attack. Joab and his men then returned to Jerusalem to the king. (20:22)

Soon thereafter there was a famine that lasted three years, and David prayed to Yahweh for guidance. Yahweh said, "It is for Saul and his bloody house, for he put to death the Gibeonites, whom he had promised to leave unharmed." (21:1)

David immediately asked the Gibeonites what he could do to atone for the sins of Saul. They said, "Let seven of Saul's descendants be given to us, and we will hang them in Gibeah." The king said, "I will do as you ask." But David spared Mephibosheth, the son of Jonathan the son of Saul, because of the oath that was between David and Jonathan. (21:2–21:7)

But David delivered seven other descendants of Saul into the hands of the Gibeonites, and they hanged them in the mountain before Yahweh. The men were put to death at the beginning of the barley harvest. Rizpah, the mother of two of the men, put their bodies on a cloth and kept the animals away even as the skies began to rain. (21:8–21:10)

David was told what Rizpah, the concubine of Saul, had done. David went and took the bones of Saul and Jonathan, which had been rescued from the Philistines after they were killed in Gilboa, and he brought them along with the bones of the seven hanged men to the land of Benjamin where they were buried in the tomb of Saul's father. After that, God was asked to have mercy on the land. (21:11–21:14)

The Philistines again attacked Israel, and David went with his army to fight them. But being old now, David grew faint, and Ishbibenob, who was a giant, almost killed David with a spear so large that the spearhead alone weighed over seven pounds. However, Abishai came to his aid and struck the Philistine and killed him. Then the men of David came to him, saying, "You shall go no more out with us to battle, otherwise you could be destroyed and Israel with you." (21:15–21:17)

This battle was followed by another with the Philistines at Gob, where two more giants were killed. Then there was another battle at Gath, where a giant who had six fingers on every hand and six toes on every foot defied Israel. Jonathan the son of Shimei, David's brother, killed him. These four giants were all brothers who fell to the soldiers of David. (21:18–21:22)

David spoke to Yahweh a song that began like this: "Yahweh is my rock, my fortress, and my deliverer. In Him I will take refuge, my shield, and the horn of my salvation. I will call on Yahweh, who is worthy to be praised. So shall I be saved from my enemies." (22:1–22:4)

Again the anger of Yahweh was kindled against Israel, and he told David to count the men of Israel capable of serving in the army. David told Joab, "Go back and forth through all the tribes of Israel from Dan even to Beersheba and count the men of fighting age." Joab said to the king, "I pray that Yahweh grant you an army one hundred times larger than it is even now, but why does my lord the king delight in this thing?" (24:1–24:3)

David insisted that Joab do as God commanded, and the captains of the army went over the Jordan and encamped in Aroer, then they went to Jazer, then Gilead, then the land of Tahtim Hodshi, then Dan Jaan, Sidon, Tyre, the cities of the Hivites, and of the Canaanites; finally, they went to the south of Judah, to Beersheba. They returned to Jerusalem at the end of nine months and twenty days. (24:4–24:8)

Joab came to David and told him that there were in Israel eight hundred thousand valiant men who drew the sword and another five hundred thousand men of Judah. David's heart struck him after hearing how many men were now in Israel. David said to Yahweh, "I have sinned greatly in that which I have done. But now, Yahweh, I beg you to forgive my foolishness." (24:9–24:10)

When David rose up in the morning, Yahweh sent the prophet Gad to David. He said to David, "Yahweh offers you three things from which you must choose: seven years of famine across the land, or will you flee three months before your foes while they pursue you, or shall there be three days of pestilence in your land?" David said to Gad, "I am in distress." Finally, David left it to Yahweh to choose. (24:11–24:14)

So Yahweh sent a pestilence on Israel for three days. From Dan to Beersheba, seventy thousand men died. When the angel stretched out his hand toward Jerusalem to destroy it, Yahweh said to the angel, "It is enough. Now stay your hand." The angel of Yahweh was by the threshing floor of Araunah the Jebusite. (24:15–24:16)

David spoke to Yahweh when he saw the angel and said, "Behold, I have sinned, and I have done perversely, but the people who follow me, what have they done? Please let your hand be against me." Gad came that day to David and said to him, "Go up, build an altar to Yahweh on the threshing floor of Araunah the Jebusite." David did as Yahweh commanded. (24:17–24:19)

Araunah bowed before the king, and David said to him, "I wish to buy your threshing floor to build an altar to Yahweh, that the plague may be stopped from afflicting the people." Araunah said to David, "Let my lord take all he wishes as a gift." The king said to Araunah, "No, I will not offer burnt offerings to Yahweh my God which cost me nothing." So David bought the threshing floor and the oxen for fifty shekels of silver. (24:20–24:24)

David built an altar to Yahweh there, and he offered burnt offerings and peace offerings, and the plague was stayed from Israel. (24:25)

MAP

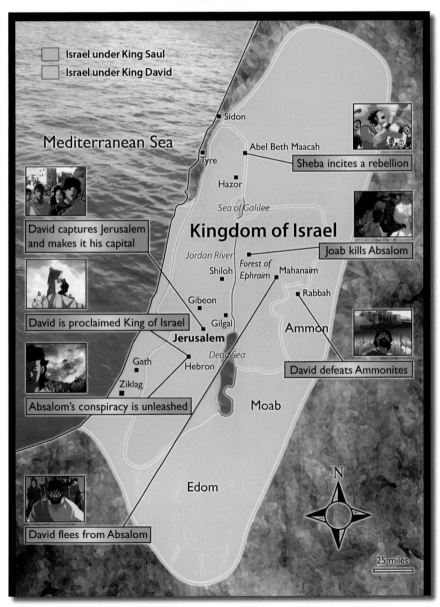

Israel under King Saul

Israel under King David

Mediterranean Sea

Sidon

Abel Beth Maacah

Tyre

Sheba incites a rebellion

Hazor

Sea of Galilee

Kingdom of Israel

David captures Jerusalem and makes it his capital

Jordan River

Forest of Ephraim

Joab kills Absalom

Shiloh

Mahanaim

Gibeon

Rabbah

David is proclaimed King of Israel

Gilgal

Jerusalem

Ammon

Dead Sea

Gath

Hebron

Ziklag

David defeats Ammonites

Absalom's conspiracy is unleashed

Moab

N

Edom

David flees from Absalom

25 miles

Join the club today and enjoy the site with our books!

THE ALMIGHTY BIBLE club

Jumpstart the Power of Prayer in Your Family!

The Family that Prays Together, Stays Together.

The Almighty Prayer Garden brings your prayers to life!

Our Family

Our Family

Say Prayer

Share Prayer

Edit Prayer

Enter Journal

Move Plant

Answered

Remove Prayer

PRAYER SELECTED

Plant Your Prayer Seed!

Time to garden! When you click on Plant My Seed, your garden will appear. Move your cursor ove it and select the spot!

Plant My Seed

WRITE YOUR PRAYER

Dear Father, help us to remember how thankful we are to know You and be loved by You.

CONTINUE

Plant prayers together with your family!

Say your prayers with your family each day!

Share your prayers with all your friends!

Take your faith to the next level at www.AlmightyBibleClub.com!

Plant your prayers. Say your prayers. Share your prayers.

THE ALMIGHTY BIBLE club

The Almighty Prayer Garden plus our incredible games bring the whole Bible to life!

Go online now and sign up for a FREE trial of fun and spiritual growth for your kids!

www.AlmightyBibleClub.com

Feel the exciting times with Paul in Rome, AD 63.

The Mission helps kids learn and experience Church history!

The Almighty Prayer Garden helps families pray together and share prayers with friends.

See your prayers come alive!

Collect hundreds of Almighty Trading Cards and use them to pass challenges in the Mission!

Collect Almighty Trading cards!

The entire family has fun and is encouraged while learning the Bible together.

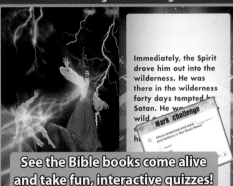

See the Bible books come alive and take fun, interactive quizzes!

"WOW. Here's an amazing way to engage kids in the Bible."
- ChildrensMinistryOnline.com